Olympic National Park
impressions

photography by James Randklev

FARCOUNTRY
PRESS

Above: Marymere Falls drops into its lush grotto.
Facing page: Western redcedars along the popular Barnes Creek Trail.
Page 4: A seastack catches a winter storm in one of the photographer's early works.
Page 5: Low tide on La Push Beach.
Title page: The scenic road to Hurricane Ridge.
Front cover: Along Sol Duc Falls Trail.
Back cover: Deer grazing along Big Meadow are a common sight at Hurricane Ridge in the summer.

Photographs by Art Wolfe appear on pages 12, 27, 49, 74
Photograph by Rod Barbee appears on page 23

ISBN 1-56037-203-6

Photographs © by James Randklev except as noted above
© 2002 Farcountry Press

Created, produced, and designed in the United States. Printed in Korea.

Endless Cycle

In the western skies storm clouds gathered over the Pacific as the changing tide forced the incoming surf over the driftwood-strewn beach at the little fishing village of La Push. I had come to photograph the storm that was fetching in from the west with high winds and pounding surf. There on the shoreline the wild foam was surging in toward the highest tide line and beyond, making a dangerous footing for my tripod and camera. The swirling fog drew close around the distant seastacks and masked the trees along the shoreline in wind-blown spray. Small boats that had been fishing on the ocean were now seeking the shelter of the docks upriver from the wild waves.

Borne on the winds, the clouds overhead skimmed the tall trees clustered along the shoreline. They were heading inland toward the Hoh Rain Forest to dampen the ancient cedars and spruce, which stood in silent groves hung with lichens and mosses. Perhaps some of those trees would fall in this storm to make way for new growth in the eternal cycle of life. The relentless wind would reach them soon, I thought, but it was now bringing the salt spray that was stinging my face. Diligently I focused my camera lens on the seastack hoping to capture the moment.

I was born and raised on the Olympic Peninsula. To a young boy this wild landscape of mountains and sea was a small paradise of discovery. My curiosity for the natural world flourished, and countless hours were spent feeding my sense of wonder. Like Tom Sawyer's, my life was a series of small adventures, without the urban distractions most kids experience. I had traveled far since then, but had come back here to photograph the beauty of this unique area. This storm was a culmination of a dream for me, for I had never captured on film the shoreline like this—with the wind and surf churning against the

rugged seastack. Little did I know this experience would launch a lifelong career in photography.

As I returned home that day, the clouds surged to pass over the deep cold waters of Lake Crescent. I could see their low, gray shapes as I drove the winding roadway along the lush forested shoreline. The chill in the air told me that winter had arrived on this Pacific storm. Regardless of what the calendar says, nature has its own way of communicating that message. Cooling and ascending, the storm's moisture was condensing into thick cumuli shapes as the front moved high into the mountains. When I reached home in Port Angeles, the evening ferryboat from Victoria was docking at the pier, and the first rain began to fall in the last light of day. The twinkling lights that ringed Ediz Hook were masked by gusts of wind-driven rain and mist. Into the night the house windows shook as the storm released its fury.

When I awoke in the red light of dawn, the Olympic Mountains glistened with newly-fallen snow. The Pacific storm had moved on to the east and the November sky was cloudless and serene. The weather, so unpredictable in this area, had surprised me once again. I was eager to experience this first snowfall in the Olympics. I anxiously waited for the park service road crew to clear the highway to Hurricane Ridge, a popular alpine destination.

The view of Mount Olympus and the Bailey Range seemed to dissolve before me into distant and receding shades of blue as the heavy wet snow began to melt under the brilliant rays of the morning sun. Meltwater was trickling beneath the crusted snow at my feet as it seeped ever downward, seeking lower elevations. In the distance, countless waterfalls and rapids released their sounds of thunder on the morning winds. Far below me the Elwha ran north toward the Strait of Juan de Fuca. To the west, the waters of the Hoh, flowing from the glaciers on Mount Olympus, ran toward the Pacific shore and returned to the source once again.

I knew at that moment I had seen, in the space of a few hours, a small portion of the endless cycle that has shaped this landscape since time began. This was the ultimate journey taken by that moisture in its many forms to return to the great source of all waters. I remembered my summer as a park ranger at Kalaloch Beach when I sat beside the fire and read the words of John Muir who wrote in his book, *Steep Trails*:

> This grand show is eternal.
> It is always sunrise somewhere,
> The dew is never all dried at once,
> > a shower is forever falling,
> > vapor is ever rising.
> Eternal sunrise, eternal sunset,
> > eternal dawn and gloaming,
> > on sea and continents and islands,
> > each in its turn
> > as the round earth rolls.

I continue to return to my beloved Olympics to experience all the diversity and beauty this National Park has to offer. This portfolio of images represents my impressions of this rugged landscape where the mountains meet the sea.

James Randklev

Olympic National Park is recognized by UNESCO as a World Biosphere Reserve and World Heritage Site.

Above: Moss-covered maples center a grove of alders and ferns.

Facing page: In Heart O' the Hills, a perfect cool mountain stream.

Above: In the upper Elwha River Valley, dogwood and vine maple in autumn.

Facing page: Growing from lichen-covered rocks in the Deer Park area, Flett violets are indigenous only to Olympic National Park.

Above: A winter storm clears off Heart O' the Hills.

Facing page: Amidst mussels, barnacles and a sea urchin shell, a blood starfish awaits incoming tide.

Above: Black bears are among the larger wild mammals that make their home in the park.

Right: Hikers pause to enjoy the beauty of Sol Duc River Falls.

Following pages: Seastacks dwarf visitors at driftwood-strewn Rialto Beach.

Above: Dating from 1926, Lake Quinault Lodge in Olympic National Forest (just outside the park) has ninety-two rooms but nary a telephone, radio, or television in them.

Left: Avalanche lilies adorn an alpine meadow near Obstruction Point.

Left: Sunset at La Push Beach.

Below: Fireweed in bloom below Hurricane Ridge.

Above: Alders along the shore of glacially-carved Lake Crescent.

Right: Queets River Rain Forest's ferns, maples and mosses make up a maritime rainforest environment.

Left: The Elwha River breaks into white water.

Below: Hurricane Ridge offers spectacular alpine views.

Right: Sweeping view of the extremely deep Lake Crescent, as seen from Mount Storm King.

Below: Evergreen forests below Deer Park.

Above: The Roosevelt elk lives in the Hoh Rain Forest.

Left: Misty greens of vine maples and sword ferns along Barnes Creek Trail.

Above: Driftwood sculpture decorates Rialto Beach.

Right: Kalaloch Creek meets the Pacific Ocean at Kalaloch Beach.

Above: Invitation to sit a spell at Lake Crescent Lodge cabins.

Left: Seasonal stream deep in Heart O' the Hills.

Above: Atop Kalaloch Beach's bluffs stand spruce trees twisted into fantastic shapes by Pacific storms.

Right. Sunset and fog combine to lend an eerie color to the Ruby Beach landscape.

Above: Rialto Beach.

Facing page: The subalpine monkeyflower flourishes along Royal Creek.

Above: Still life of gull feather among beach grass and driftwood, Cape Alava.

Facing page: Mountain ash offers its bright berries on the park's eastern side.

Above: Snow-flocked tree atop Hurricane Ridge.

Right: Reflections in a subalpine lake of Royal Basin.

Fog rolls in among Heart O' the Hills' hemlocks and firs.

Above: Kalaloch Lodge's "auto cabins" and hotel were constructed during the 1920s and 1930s.

Right: Goldenrod flowers among driftwood logs along La Push Beach.

Above: Wind-drawn snow patterns on Hurricane Ridge.

Left: Seagulls pause for relaxation and preening on Point of Arches Beach.

Above: Mountain heather survives in adverse conditions.

Right: Summer snowmelt feeds Twin Falls in the 5,000-foot-high Royal Basin.

Hiking through the Hall of Mosses in Hoh Rain Forest, a protected part of the temperate rain forest that stretches from Northern California to Alaska

Northern spotted owls live in the park's old-growth forests.

Above: A small stream in the Sol Duc River Valley.

Right: Dewdrops on a spider web in Hoh Rain Forest.

Above: Vine maples and ferns with Western redcedar.

Facing page: Treasures on the beach.

Above: A nurse log provides nutrients for other plants like these brackett fungi.

Facing page: Fading sun at La Push Beach.

Above: Frost touches the Elwha River Valley.

Right: Park visitors explore Ruby Beach.

Above: Cedar bough symmetry.

Facing page: Bears and deer are often seen along Deer Lake, part of the high-elevation Seven Lakes Basin.

Above: Maple trees' autumn color brightens the upper Elwha River Valley.

Right: Seagulls share Rialto Beach at sundown.

Facing page: Popular foot trail passes through a Sol Duc Valley alder grove.

Below: Cascades in the Royal Basin plume into "horsetails."

Above: Lake Crescent as seen from the lodge's inviting porch.

Facing page: Lupine rises in an alpine meadow near Obstruction Point Road.

Above: Black-tailed deer, Hurricane Ridge.

Right: Wildflowers bloom along the alpine meadows of Obstruction Point.

Above: Backpackers along Shi Shi Beach and the Point of Arches.

Left: Twilight over seastacks at La Push Beach.

Right: Moss-covered maples and evergreens along mountain stream at La Poel, Lake Crescent.

Below: Queets Rain Forest can receive 150 inches of rain annually.

Above: Devil's club grows along the Marymere Falls Trail.

Facing page: Tide runnels at Shi Shi Beach.

Facing page: The sun room at historic Lake Crescent Lodge.

Below: An Olympic marmot mother and babies check to see whether danger is in the air.

Panorama of the Olympic Mountains in the park's northern reaches.

Above: Grand Lake and Valley, back country.

Left. Gray Wolf Ridge and the Needles from Deer Park area.

James Randklev

Master landscape photographer James Randklev has photographed America for thirty years, primarily with a large-format camera that provides the rich images collected in this volume. His brilliant and sensitive work has made him one of the Sierra Club's most published photographers. His color photographs have appeared in books, periodicals, and advertising—and have been exhibited in shows in the United States and abroad. In 1997, he was the sole American chosen to exhibit in the International Exhibition of Nature Photography in Evian, France. His previous books are: *In Nature's Heart: The Wilderness Days of John Muir; Georgia: Images of Wildness; Wild and Scenic Florida; Georgia Impressions;* and *Georgia Simply Beautiful.*